Usborne

First Sticker Book

Diggers

Illustrated by Dan Crisp

Contents

There are lots of digger stickers at the back of this book for you to stick on each page.

Words by Sam Taplin

Designed by Meg Dobbie and Matt Durber

Making a road

There are lots of busy diggers working here. Excavators and front loaders are digging up a road, while road graders and pavers are making a new one.

ROAD CLOSED

At the quarry

Front loaders and excavators are scooping up heavy rocks and carrying them away from the quarry.

At the building site

Bulldozers are flattening the ground at the building site, and excavators are digging holes where the buildings will go.

In the forest

Log loaders and claw diggers are carrying away trees that have been chopped down in the forest.

At the farm

Front loaders and hedge trimmers are working on the farm.

At the demolition site

Huge diggers called long reach excavators are smashing the old buildings at the demolition site.

Under the ground

Roadheaders with spiky blades are cutting tunnels deep under the ground. Big drilling machines are making holes in the surface.

At the dump

Scrap-handlers are crushing old cars at the dump, and bulldozers are sorting the other waste into different heaps.

14

Make your own picture

Use the stickers to make your
own picture on this page.